Original title:
Mending My Heart

Copyright © 2024 Swan Charm
All rights reserved.

Author: Paulina Pähkel
ISBN HARDBACK: 978-9916-89-859-8
ISBN PAPERBACK: 978-9916-89-860-4
ISBN EBOOK: 978-9916-89-861-1

## A Journey into Forgiveness

In the quiet of the heart's embrace,
We seek the light, a gentle space.
Wounds that bind, begin to mend,
On this path, love is our friend.

In the shadow of our past mistakes,
Grace whispers softly, the silence breaks.
With every step, the burden fades,
In the hands of mercy, hope cascades.

Forgiveness blooms like flowers rare,
Transforming sorrow into prayer.
For in surrender, we find release,
A sacred bond that grants us peace.

Let not the pain define our soul,
For every wound can make us whole.
In unity, we rise above,
Charting courses paved with love.

A journey shared, with spirits soar,
In faith, we find what we live for.
With open hearts, we forge ahead,
In forgiveness, our spirits are fed.

## Where the Spirit Finds Rest

Beneath the stars, our dreams take flight,
In divine presence, we see the light.
Where worries cease and fears dissolve,
The spirit seeks what can resolve.

In whispered prayers, our hearts align,
Finding solace, pure and divine.
A sanctuary of holy peace,
Where burdens cast, and worries cease.

Through trials faced, we stand as one,
With open arms, our journey begun.
In this haven, we renew our trust,
With faith as steadfast as ancient dust.

Each moment cherished, each breath a gift,
The spirit's journey, a gentle lift.
In stillness found, the soul is blessed,
In sacred calm, the heart finds rest.

So let us gather in love's embrace,
Finding comfort in each other's grace.
For where love flows, the spirit thrives,
In unity, true joy derives.

## Echoes of Love's True Calling

In the silence, hear the call,
Love's gentle whisper, touching all.
In every heartbeat, shadows fade,
When kindness lights the path we've made.

A melody of hearts that sing,
In union wrapped, our spirits cling.
Through trials faced, we rise anew,
In love's embrace, we renew the true.

The echoes of compassion ring,
A sacred bond that life will bring.
In every moment, grace we find,
The threads of love will always bind.

With open eyes, we see the grace,
In every soul, a warm embrace.
Through acts of kindness, truth unfolds,
In love's pure light, our story holds.

Let every voice harmonize in song,
For love is where our hearts belong.
With each connection, a purpose clear,
In echoes of love, we persevere.

## Transcending Sorrow with Hope


In the valleys where shadows creep,
We search for light, our souls to keep.
Transcending sorrow, we rise above,
With hearts united, we find our love.

Each tear that falls, a seed of grace,
In every struggle, a cherished place.
With faith as fuel, we journey on,
Through darkest nights, we seek the dawn.

Hope like a river flows through time,
Washing away what feels like crime.
In pain's embrace, we learn to grow,
Resilience blooms, and spirits glow.

Together standing, hand in hand,
With love as guide, we'll make our stand.
Each step of faith, each heart restored,
Transforms our sorrow, a sacred sword.

In the tapestry of life we weave,
Woven with hope, we dare believe.
For in each trial, there lies a sign,
That sorrow passed, brings joy divine.

## Cherubic Blessings of the Past

In the garden where angels tread,
Whispers of heaven softly spread.
Stars align in sacred grace,
Guiding our steps in sacred space.

Little hearts in joyful prayer,
Reach for love that's always there.
Cherubs dance on timeless beams,
Filling our lives with gentle dreams.

Moments cherished, forever bright,
Shining through the dark of night.
In faith we find the light of old,
Stories of peace that can be told.

Memories wrapped in warm embrace,
Echoes of hope we now trace.
Hand in hand, we walk this path,
In love's presence, we shall last.

## **Restoration in Divine Love**

In the stillness, a voice we hear,
Calling softly, drawing near.
Hearts once broken, now in bloom,
God's gentle touch dispels all gloom.

Wounds are healed with sacred grace,
Every tear, a holy trace.
From the ashes, we will rise,
Renewed spirit, the soul's reprise.

In unity, we lift our song,
Finding where we all belong.
Love binds us in its tender thread,
In faith's embrace, we shall be led.

In each dawn, a promise made,
In the light, our fears will fade.
Together in this holy dance,
We restore our souls' advance.

## The Promise of Resilience

From the storm, we find our way,
Guided by the light of day.
Though we falter, we won't break,
In the trials, our hearts awake.

Rooted strong in loving grace,
Faithward journeys we embrace.
Every struggle, a chance to grow,
In darkness, our courage will glow.

When shadows seem to darken skies,
Hope arises, it never dies.
With whispered prayers, we stand as one,
In resilience, our victory won.

In love's arms, we shall remain,
Finding joy within the pain.
The promise of life's endless flow,
Is found in every tear we sow.

## **Faithful Echoes of the Heart**

In silence, hear the echoes bound,
Faithful whispers, grace profound.
Every heartbeat sings the song,
Of love's journey, deep and long.

When we gather, spirits soar,
Hands entwined, we seek for more.
In devotion, our stories blend,
Creating warmth that will not end.

Through the trials, we lift our gaze,
Finding light in faith's bright blaze.
The heart's yearning, a sacred chart,
Forging bonds that will not part.

With every step on this shared road,
We carry love, our greatest load.
In faithful echoes, peace impart,
Uniting voices, soul to heart.

## The Soul's Renovation

In quiet grove, the spirit sings,
With open heart, the promise brings.
A light descends, the shadows flee,
In grace renewed, we wander free.

The old is cast, the new is born,
With every breath, a hope reborn.
The past a whisper, softly fades,
And in His love, our fear invades.

Through trials faced, our strength made whole,
With faith we rise, the journey's goal.
In sacred trust, our dreams align,
A tapestry of love divine.

With every step, the path revealed,
An open heart, our wounds shall yield.
In prayerful echoes, we ascend,
The soul's own voice, our truest friend.

## Beneath the Cross of Sorrow

Beneath the weight, the burdens lay,
In silent tears, we find our way.
A hand extended, grace bestowed,
In darkest night, His light bestowed.

Each thorn a mark of love divine,
In suffering's grip, a hope we find.
The warmth of faith, a guiding light,
In every shadow, shines so bright.

The echoes of redemption call,
In gentle whispers, holding all.
Our sorrows shared, we stand as one,
Beneath the cross, a victory won.

With lifted hearts, we rise anew,
In sacred trust, we journey through.
Each step in love, a promise old,
In God's own hands, our lives unfold.

## The Cloak of Divine Embrace

Wrapped in the cloak of mercy's grace,
In every trial, we find our place.
With arms enkindled, love surrounds,
In whispered prayers, His voice abounds.

The fabric woven, spirit strong,
In unity we sing our song.
Each thread a story, rich and rare,
In every heart, His presence there.

The warmth of faith, a gentle guide,
With courage bold, we face the tide.
In every moment, peace takes flight,
With each embrace, darkness turns to light.

Through valleys deep, our souls adorned,
We rise refreshed, our hearts reborn.
In love we dwell, together face,
The beauty found in divine grace.

## **The Pilgrim's Heart Restored**

A pilgrim's heart, with steps redefined,
Through trials faced, we seek and find.
With dusty feet, we walk the way,
In every moment, hope holds sway.

The road of faith, a winding track,
With whispers soft, we won't look back.
In sacred signs, our spirits soar,
With every dawn, we're called to more.

The journey long, yet sweet the prize,
In love's embrace, the spirit flies.
With every prayer, a path made clear,
In light and truth, we draw Him near.

From brokenness to wholeness wrought,
In every lesson, wisdom taught.
The pilgrim's heart shall ever beat,
With grace renewed, we stand complete.

## Light Breaking Through

In the stillness of the night,
A whisper calls my name,
Light begins to break forth,
Casting aside all shame.

Hope rekindles in my heart,
As shadows melt away,
Guided by the sacred flame,
I find the strength to stay.

With each dawn that gently breaks,
The world is born anew,
A promise wrapped in His grace,
Drenched in morning dew.

Here in the warmth of love's embrace,
I stand without a fear,
For the light that shines within,
Will always draw me near.

Through valleys deep and mountains high,
His guiding hand I seek,
In the light that breaks through dark,
I find the joy I speak.

## A New Dawn's Promise

As the night begins to fade,
A promise starts to rise,
Hope unfurls like morning's bloom,
Beneath the waking skies.

Each ray that kisses tender earth,
Brings warmth to frigid air,
A sign that love will conquer all,
In faith, I choose to share.

With every heartbeat, I rejoice,
His mercy flowing free,
In the dawn's embrace, I trust,
He walks along with me.

The shadows of my troubled past,
Are washed away in light,
With every step upon this path,
I flourish in His might.

In the splendor of this day,
New journeys I will find,
For in the dawn of every morn,
Hope's promise is defined.

## Beneath the Stars of Providence

Underneath the vast expanse,
Where stars like blessings gleam,
I find my soul's tranquility,
In every whispered dream.

Celestial bodies shining bright,
Guardians of the night,
They tell of faith unfailing,
In shadows, there's a light.

Each twinkle speaks of destiny,
A map of love divine,
With every breath I take anew,
I trust, I am aligned.

The cosmos spins a tapestry,
Of hope and peace combined,
In silence, I feel His presence,
A love so sweet, so kind.

Beneath the stars, I lift my heart,
In prayers that softly rise,
For in this vast universe,
His wisdom never lies.

## **The Dance of the Redeemed**

In the sanctuary of the soul,
A melody plays true,
The dance of joy, the dance of grace,
In every step I do.

With hands uplifted skyward,
I feel the Spirit's flow,
Together in this holy rite,
We conquer all below.

Every twirl, a testament,
Of battles fought and won,
With every rhythm of my heart,
I sing to Him, the One.

In this dance that knows no bounds,
Freedom fills the air,
For we are called the redeemed,
In His love, stripped bare.

So let us dance with fervent joy,
And sing a heavenly tune,
For in this sacred dance of life,
We rise like morning's moon.

## The Hopeful Wound

In shadows deep, the spirit weeps,
Yet faith ignites, a light that keeps.
A wound may ache, but hope will rise,
With every breath, toward the skies.

In pain's embrace, the soul will yearn,
For healing's touch, a flame that burns.
Each tear a prayer, each sigh a song,
In gentle whispers, we belong.

Though scars may linger, love will mend,
In every crack, new life transcends.
The hope within our hearts will bloom,
Emerging from the darkest gloom.

With faith as guide, we journey on,
Through trials faced, a dawn is born.
The hopeful wound, a sacred space,
In suffering, we find His grace.

So let us rise, our spirits soar,
For through the pain, we seek much more.
The promise held, though trembling hands,
In love's embrace, our strength expands.

## Cadence of a Healing Heart

In rhythmic beats, the heart will mend,
A sacred song that will not end.
Each pulse a prayer, each throb a peace,
In harmony, the soul's release.

Through darkest nights, the stars will sing,
The cadence soft, a gentle thing.
With every breath, we draw anew,
The strength to rise, the light breaks through.

Wounds find solace in whispered grace,
A healing touch in time and space.
We move in faith, with hope entwined,
The heart's rhythm, divinely aligned.

The journey long, yet no retreat,
For in each step, the Spirit meets.
With open hearts, we learn to trust,
In every challenge, our faith is just.

So let the rhythm guide our way,
In love's embrace, we'll humbly sway.
The cadence of a healing heart,
A testament that won't depart.

## Resilient Blossoms in the Garden

In fields of grace, where flowers bloom,
Resilient hearts dispel the gloom.
With roots held firm, despite the storm,
In unity, we find our form.

Each petal soft, a story told,
Of trials faced and courage bold.
Through seasons' change, we stand in line,
Resilient blossoms, a design divine.

Though winds may howl and shadows creep,
The garden's heart is ours to keep.
In every color, every scent,
A tapestry of love is meant.

We nourish dreams with faith's pure rain,
In every flower, a joy, a pain.
Together we rise, hand in hand,
In this sacred, garden land.

Amidst the weeds, we find our way,
With hope as sun, we'll greet the day.
Resilient blossoms, ever bright,
In God's embrace, we take our flight.

## A Tapestry of Grace Unfurled

In threads of faith, the story weaves,
A tapestry of grace that cleaves.
With every stitch, a lesson learned,
In love's embrace, our hearts are turned.

Each color bold, a truth revealed,
In trials faced, our wounds are healed.
With gentle hands, we craft and mold,
The fabric shines, a sight to behold.

Through valleys low, on mountains high,
We find our strength, we learn to fly.
In moments dark, we seek the light,
The woven threads hold us so tight.

As life unfolds, the pattern grows,
In every thread, our spirit knows.
A tapestry rich, with stories spun,
In harmony, we are made one.

So let us cherish every line,
In grace's flow, our hearts entwine.
A tapestry of love unfurled,
In every soul, a new world.

## **The Light After the Storm**

Through darkened skies the thunder roars,
Yet faith remains, it ever soars.
The tempest fades, the calm returns,
In shattered hearts, the spirit learns.

Like diamonds bright, the raindrops gleam,
In trials passed, we find our dream.
The sun will rise, the shadows flee,
In every storm, there's hope to see.

With every gust, our strength is tried,
Yet love renews, we will not hide.
The world may break, but we will stand,
In gentle light, we hold God's hand.

So lift your eyes, behold the dawn,
Embrace the light, let fear be gone.
The storm may rage, but hearts will mend,
For every end, there is a friend.

## **Blessed are the Broken-Hearted**

Blessed are they who mourn in pain,
For in their tears, grace will reign.
The heart once shattered, now made whole,
Transcends the loss, revives the soul.

From ashes rise, the spirits soar,
In quietude, they find the door.
To love again, to learn anew,
In brokenness, we see what's true.

Each scar a story, each wound a song,
In gentle whispers, we belong.
With faith restored, we walk in light,
For every heart can find its flight.

So let the broken feel the grace,
In every tear, a sacred place.
They carry love, forever blessed,
In tender hearts, we find our rest.

## **Faith's Embrace in Times of Darkness**

In shadows deep, where fear may dwell,
We find the light, our hearts compel.
With faith as guide, we rise anew,
In darkest nights, love sees us through.

The trials steep, the paths unclear,
But trust in God will calm our fear.
In every doubt, His promise stands,
Through faith's embrace, we take His hands.

Each burden shared will lighten load,
In every storm, we walk God's road.
With whispers soft, hope breaks the night,
In faith we stand, in love's pure light.

So hold your hearts, and lift your prayer,
For in His care, we find our share.
Through every storm, we learn to praise,
In faith's embrace, our spirits blaze.

# **Radiant Heart, Resilient Spirit**

In trials faced, the heart shall shine,
With every wound, we are divine.
Resilient spirits rise above,
In darkest days, we learn to love.

With every tear, a lesson learned,
In gentle strength, the spirit turned.
Through burdens shared, our hope will gleam,
In radiant grace, we find our dream.

With courage found in silent prayer,
We lift our hearts, our burdens bare.
The light within will guide our way,
In every night, we greet the day.

So shine your light, through thick and thin,
With steadfast hearts, we rise again.
Resilient souls, forever bright,
In love and faith, we claim our right.

## Illuminated by Hope's Flame

In the night, a flicker shines,
Guiding hearts with sacred signs.
With every breath, the spirit soars,
Hope's embrace forever pours.

Through the darkness, love will lead,
Nurturing every fragile seed.
Faith ignites the dimmest place,
A warm and radiant grace.

Though trials may cloud the way,
Hope's light beckons, bright as day.
Together, we rise, we stand,
Unified by a guiding hand.

In whispers soft, the truth will call,
His presence comforts, never small.
With each flicker, our dreams take flight,
Illuminated by love's pure light.

## Rivulets of Compassion

Pour out gently, loving streams,
Sowing kindness, nurturing dreams.
In each heart, the river flows,
Bringing peace where wisdom grows.

Hands extended, hearts aligned,
In unity, our strength we find.
Together we mend the pain,
Rivulets will wash the stain.

Every tear, a sacred sign,
Flowing softly, His design.
In the currents, grace shall meet,
Mercy blooms beneath our feet.

With every touch, we break the chain,
Rising up, we feel the gain.
Compassion's flow it knows no end,
In His love, we all transcend.

## Songs of Reconciliation

Let us raise a joyful song,
Where all hearts and souls belong.
In harmony, we seek the way,
Together brighter, come what may.

Voices merge like river streams,
Healing wounds, fulfilling dreams.
Forgiveness paints the canvas wide,
Renewed paths where love can guide.

In every note, a story told,
A melody of warmth unfolds.
From ashes, we shall rise anew,
In grace, we weave a vibrant hue.

Through the storms, we sing and pray,
Uniting souls, dispelling gray.
With every chord, past pains undone,
Songs of love, forever won.

## Embracing the Light Within


Deep within, a beacon glows,
In quiet whispers, wisdom flows.
Embracing truths that we hold dear,
The light within frees every fear.

With open hearts, we seek to find,
The sacred spark that intertwines.
In silence, revelations bloom,
Illumined paths dispel the gloom.

Each step taken, a dance divine,
In His presence, we brightly shine.
With faith as cloak, we journey far,
Guided always by His star.

Together, let our spirits soar,
Unlocking doors to love and more.
Embrace the light, let it be known,
In every heart, He calls us home.

## Hope's Verses in Despair

In shadows deep, where sorrows wane,
A flicker shines through heavy rain.
Though darkness seems to hold its reign,
The heart holds fast, it knows no chain.

Each tear a seed, in mourning sown,
From grief arise the strength we've grown.
With whispered prayers, the spirit's tone,
In quiet faith, we're never alone.

When doubts like thunder cloud our sight,
The stars still gleam in the endless night.
For every storm, there's dawn's sweet light,
In every loss, we find our fight.

In every trial, a lesson waits,
In brokenness, the soul creates.
What once was lost, the heart regenerates,
With every breath, our spirit elevates.

So hold your dreams, let them inspire,
Through shattered paths, ignite the fire.
In whispered hope, the heart conspire,
To rise again, as we desire.

## Ascending from Heartache's Depths

From ashes cold, a soul takes flight,
In darkest hours, we seek the light.
With every tear, a path ignites,
Towards healing's grace, our spirit's height.

In silence, we find strength anew,
With faith in heart, we'll push on through.
Though heavy burdens lie in view,
In love's embrace, we are made true.

The weight of loss, a heavy cloak,
Yet in each word, a soft hope spoke.
Resilience blooms from shattered yoke,
Through fractured lines, our hearts invoke.

With each new dawn, the sun will rise,
Transforming pain into wise ties.
With steadfast faith, we'll touch the skies,
And find our strength in whispered sighs.

So here's to dreams that soar above,
In darkest night, we learn to love.
From heartache's depths, we rise like doves,
With grace profound, we sing of love.

## Whispers of Renewal

In quiet moments, shadows meet,
A promise waits, though dreams deplete.
With gentle breath, the heart skips beat,
In whispers soft, our souls find heat.

From barren lands, a flower blooms,
In spite of winter's harshest dooms.
With every breath, the spirit consumes,
The light that flickers, never looms.

Awake, O heart, from slumber deep,
In troubles vast, the soul must leap.
For in the night, the stars we keep,
Lead us to shores where dreams don't sleep.

Within each struggle, a treasure lies,
Beneath the weight, a new sunrise.
For every tear, a guiding prize,
In softest whispers, hope replies.

So rise again, with courage blessed,
In moments small, we are caressed.
Through every trial, we are confessed,
In whispers sweet, we find our rest.

## **Grace Beyond the Fracture**

In broken pieces, light does gleam,
Through cracks of heart lies hope's pure beam.
Within the pain, we chase the dream,
In fractured flaws, our spirits team.

Each wound a story, wisdom shares,
In deepest trials, compassion flares.
As we collect our scattered prayers,
In grace we walk, unburdened cares.

Though shadows loom and fears may rise,
The heart holds fast from darkened skies.
For in each breath, the spirit ties,
A tapestry of love that flies.

With every heartbeat, the journey flows,
In laughter's song, the spirit knows.
Through every storm, the wisdom grows,
From grace we gather, the heart bestows.

So let us rise and dance anew,
From fractures bold, creation's hue.
With open hearts, our vision true,
In grace beyond, we find the view.

# Grace's Gentle Repair

In shadows deep, where sorrows dwell,
God's hand descends, a soothing spell.
With whispers soft, His love does flow,
Restoring souls, as rivers grow.

Each broken heart, a canvas bare,
He paints anew, with gentle care.
From ashes rise, with faith anew,
In love's embrace, we find our view.

The weight of grief, like chains, we bear,
Yet in His grace, we breathe the air.
A balm for wounds, in faith we find,
A sacred path, to peace aligned.

With every tear that falls like rain,
He gathers close, our joy and pain.
In every step, His light we trace,
Through trials faced, we find His grace.

So let us walk in cherished light,
With hope reborn, dispelling night.
For in His arms, we're made whole,
A gentle touch, renewing soul.

## **Whispers of Divine Restoration**

In quietude, the Spirit speaks,
Through whispered prayers, our hearts He seeks.
A balm of peace, for wounds laid bare,
Restoring hope, with tender care.

Each moment still, a sacred scene,
Where faith ignites, and hearts convene.
With lifted hands, we cry to Thee,
For in Thy grace, we long to be.

The mountains high, the valleys low,
In every place, Thy love do flow.
A gentle hand, on burdens placed,
In every trial, Your light embraced.

Through storms that rage, we find our rest,
In holy arms, we are blessed.
Your whispers calm, the raging sea,
In trust we stand, forever free.

So let us dwell in Spirit's care,
With open hearts, our trust declare.
For in Your hands, we are restored,
In quiet grace, forever adored.

## Threads of the Sacred Weave

In life's great tapestry, threads entwine,
Stitched with love, in a design divine.
Each color bright, each shadow cast,
A sacred story, boundless and vast.

With every thread, a tale unfolds,
Of brokenness and love retold.
With gentle hands, the weaver guides,
Through valleys deep, where joy abides.

Though frayed and worn, our fabric bears,
The marks of grace in answered prayers.
In unity, we find our strength,
In woven hearts, we span the length.

The seams of faith, so tight and true,
A crimson thread that binds us too.
Together, stitched by mercy's hand,
In love's embrace, forever stand.

So let us honor this sacred weave,
In every thread, the chance to believe.
For in His plan, we find our place,
A tapestry of endless grace.

## Healing Hands of the Almighty

With healing hands, the Savior came,
To touch the lost, to heal the lame.
In every heart, His love ignites,
Transforming darkness into lights.

Amidst our trials, storms that roar,
His hands extend, to heal and restore.
With gentle touch, the pain will cease,
In every wound, He brings us peace.

When burdens bear, and hope seems lost,
We find in Him, a love embossed.
A balm for wounds, in time of need,
In every prayer, His heart shall lead.

Through valleys low, and mountains high,
In faith we rise, on wings we fly.
For every tear, a story told,
In His embrace, we are consoled.

So let us seek His healing light,
With open hearts, we find our sight.
In every moment, trust shall grow,
For in His hands, our spirits flow.

## Redemption's Healing Touch

In shadows deep, we call to Thee,
With open hearts, set our spirits free.
Your love, a balm for wounds unseen,
In grace we rise, renewed and clean.

O gentle hands, from Heaven's grace,
Embrace our souls, in love's warm space.
Through trials faced, we find our song,
In faith we stand, where we belong.

Each tear of pain, a seed of trust,
In your embrace, we find what's just.
From ashes rise, our burdens shared,
In unity, our hearts are bared.

Let mercy flow, like rivers wide,
As paths of hope, in You we bide.
A tapestry of joy and strife,
In Your embrace, we find our life.

## Anointed by Tears of Joy

With every tear, a prayer ascends,
In sorrow deep, the heart descends.
Yet in the night, we find Your light,
Anointed souls, through faith ignite.

The veil of grief, so heavy worn,
Transforms to grace, a new day born.
In joyous weeps, redemption weaves,
Our burdens lifted, hope believes.

From depths of pain, our spirits soar,
In every tear, You're evermore.
With hearts set free, we sing anew,
In joy's embrace, we worship You.

In sacred trust, we rise above,
Surrounded always by Your love.
Each tear, a testament of grace,
Anointed by joy in this sacred space.

## Harmony from the Fragile Ashes

From fragile ashes, a hymn arises,
In brokenness, our spirit prizes.
In unity, we find our song,
A melody where we belong.

Through trials faced and battles fought,
In every lesson, wisdom's sought.
Like phoenix rising from the flame,
In faith reborn, we know Your name.

The dance of hope through darkest hours,
In fragile hearts, You plant the flowers.
With hands held high, we seek the light,
In harmony, we find the fight.

Together strong, we rise again,
In every heart, Your love we pen.
From ashes whole, our spirits sing,
In sacred union, we take wing.

## Spirit's Renewal in Distant Lands

In distant lands our spirits roam,
A journey wide but never alone.
With every step, our hearts align,
In sacred trust, Your presence shines.

The winds of change, a gentle call,
Reviving hope in us, through all.
Each sacred moment, pure and bright,
Guides us forth in faith's true light.

In valleys low and mountains high,
We walk in grace, beneath the sky.
A tapestry of love we weave,
In every breath, we learn to believe.

Through trials faced in foreign lands,
We feel Your touch, through gentle hands.
With open hearts, we share the way,
In spirit's renewal, we find our stay.

## The Sanctuary of Solace

In the quiet light of grace,
Souls find peace in a warm embrace.
Whispers of hope in every prayer,
Heaven's love lingers everywhere.

Walk on paths of faith and trust,
In sacred stones, we find what's just.
Hearts entwined in sacred beams,
Together we ascend our dreams.

Shadows fade in divine might,
Each step guided by holy light.
With every tear, a scar is healed,
In this sanctuary, love revealed.

Mountains bow, the oceans weep,
In His arms, our souls are deep.
Rest in the calm, embrace the dawn,
In solace found, our fears are gone.

Together we rise, forever blessed,
In the sanctuary, hearts find rest.
With faith as our shield, love as our sword,
In this embrace, we serve the Lord.

## **Each Beat a Divine Promise**

With every heartbeat, a vow is made,
In rhythm's pulse, our fears will fade.
Heaven's whisper, a sacred song,
In each beat, we know we belong.

Life's fleeting moments, a dance of grace,
In trials faced, we seek His face.
Each breath we take, a prayer to the sky,
In love we rise, in faith we fly.

The spirit's echo, a guiding flame,
In every heart, He knows our name.
Together we sing, as one we unite,
With each beat, we shine so bright.

Mountains tremble with our praise,
In joy we gather, forever stays.
Hands uplifted, we honor His call,
In His embrace, we rise, not fall.

Each beat a promise, steadfast, true,
In love's creation, all things new.
With hearts entwined, we walk His way,
In every beat, we live and pray.

# Rebirth Through the Celestial Winds

In the whispering winds of dawn,
We find the strength to carry on.
Wings of faith, so pure and bright,
In celestial tides, we find our light.

Casting shadows of doubt aside,
In love's embrace, we shall abide.
The earth rejoices, the heavens sing,
Through the storms, our spirits spring.

A journey marked by grace we tread,
With every step, the past is shed.
In sacred breath, we feel reborn,
In the promise of a new morn.

Hearts like phoenix rise anew,
With every trial, our strength we grew.
Together soaring, hand in hand,
In divine alleys, we take our stand.

Through celestial winds, our souls unite,
In harmonious echoes, fueled by light.
Rebirth awaits in the arms of grace,
In love's embrace, we find our place.

## Songs of the Redeemed Heart

In the chorus of the night, we sing,
Of redemption's love, the joy it brings.
Threads of mercy weave our song,
In every heart, where we belong.

Voices lifted, spirits free,
In unity, we taste the sea.
With every note, our souls ignite,
In the songs of joy, we find our light.

Shattered chains and burdens cast,
In love's embrace, we stand steadfast.
Echoes linger in the sacred air,
Songs of hope dispel despair.

With grateful hearts, we dance and pray,
In rhythmic grace, we find our way.
Each step a promise, a pledge of love,
In the songs of the heart, we rise above.

Together as one, our voices soar,
In the symphony of grace, forever more.
May our songs resound, in every part,
As we live, we share the redeemed heart.

## In Sacred Silence, I Heal

In the quiet of the night, I pray,
Whispers of peace guide my way.
In stillness, my heart finds its voice,
A gentle reminder, I rejoice.

With every breath, I feel the light,
Casting away the shadows of fright.
In sacred silence, healing flows,
A touch of grace in all that grows.

The love I seek is deep within,
A symphony of peace to begin.
With faith as my anchor, I rise,
In the warmth of the divine, I surmise.

Through trials faced, I find my strength,
In prayer, I travel endless length.
The spirit whispers, softly sings,
In sacred silence, my heart takes wing.

As dawn breaks gently, I stand renewed,
In moments of stillness, my soul is imbued.
With every heartbeat, I come to know,
In sacred silence, I heal and grow.

## The Bridge Over Troubled Waters

In the storm's embrace, I search for calm,
A bridge of faith becomes my balm.
Through troubled waters, I find my way,
A guiding light that will not sway.

With every wave that crashes near,
I gather strength, dispelling fear.
The love I cherish bridges the life,
Transforming chaos into light.

As rivers rage and torrents swell,
In the heart of struggle, I dwell.
Yet faith will guide my weary feet,
To solid ground, the path is sweet.

The bridge I walk is built on trust,
With gentle whispers, my heart adjusts.
Each step I take, I feel the grace,
In troubled waters, I find my place.

With every sunrise, hope unfolds,
The bridge grows strong as love upholds.
Together we can face the tide,
Through troubled waters, faith is our guide.

## Healing in the Embrace of Faith

In the cradle of prayer, I find my rest,
Wrapped in love, I am truly blessed.
Healing whispers fill the air,
In the embrace of faith, I lay bare.

With hands uplifted, I seek the light,
Casting away shadows of night.
The spirit mends the broken seams,
In faith's embrace, I dare to dream.

Every wound becomes a story told,
In the warmth of grace, I feel the gold.
With each heartbeat, I rise anew,
In the healing embrace, love breaks through.

The journey is long, but I walk with pride,
In faith's embrace, I will not hide.
Together we heal, like rivers that flow,
In the embrace of faith, our spirits grow.

As dawn reveals its golden hue,
In the embrace of faith, I find my crew.
With love as my compass, I journey on,
Healing in faith, I am never gone.

## Spirits United in Grace

In the tapestry of life, we weave,
A sacred bond that we believe.
Together we sing, our spirits soar,
In unity, we open heaven's door.

With every heartbeat, we align,
In the dance of grace, our souls entwine.
Whispers of love guide our quest,
In shared faith, we find our rest.

Though paths may wander, hearts stay true,
In storms of doubt, love pulls us through.
With arms wide open, we embrace the day,
Spirits united in grace, we pray.

Through trials faced, we stand as one,
In the light of truth, the battle is won.
Together we rise, not alone in fight,
In spirits united, we find our light.

As the stars align, we shine so bright,
In the heart of love, we take our flight.
With grace as our guide, we treasure the space,
Where souls connect, spirits united in grace.

# **Sacred Affirmations of Renewal**

In whispered prayers, we find our light,
Each dawn brings grace, dispelling night.
With hearts unbound, we seek the peace,
In sacred bonds, our fears release.

Through trials faced, our spirits soar,
Embracing love forevermore.
With faith as guide, our paths align,
In sacred truths, our souls entwine.

The sun will rise on every dream,
In harmony, we softly beam.
As seasons turn, we weave our fate,
In unity, we celebrate.

With open hearts, we stand as one,
In sacred acts, our journey's begun.
From ashes born, we start anew,
In sacred affirmations, we pursue.

## In Grace, We Rise

From depths of sorrow, we ascend,
In grace, we rise, our hearts unbend.
With every breath, our spirits sing,
Embracing joy that faith will bring.

The burdens lift as love draws near,
In silent strength, we banish fear.
With hands outstretched, we touch the sky,
In grace, we rise, we learn to fly.

Each step we take, a dance of light,
With trust, we walk, our souls ignite.
In circles bound by holy ties,
Together, still, in grace, we rise.

With every trial, we find our worth,
In sacred moments, we are rebirthed.
With faith as compass, we will strive,
In harmony, in grace, we thrive.

## **Stitches of Celestial Love**

In every heartbeat, love's thread we weave,
With gentle hands, we learn to believe.
Across the heavens, our voices soar,
Stitches of love bind evermore.

Through trials met, our hearts entwined,
In perfect peace, our souls aligned.
Each knot a promise, each seam a prayer,
Stitches of love, adorned with care.

With threads of faith, our quilt unfolds,
In vibrant hues, the story told.
Together strong, we mend the fray,
Stitches of love light our way.

In sacred spaces, our spirit glows,
In every touch, the love still flows.
With every stitch, our bond divine,
In stitches of celestial love, we shine.

## The Spirit's Gentle Currents

In waters deep, the spirit flows,
With gentle currents, love bestows.
Beneath the surface, whispers rise,
In every wave, a sweet surprise.

Guided by light, we drift along,
In harmony, our hearts belong.
Through trials faced, our courage found,
The spirit's currents wrap around.

In silence still, we come to know,
In currents pure, our blessings grow.
With every breath, we find our way,
The spirit's gentle touch, our stay.

So let us flow on waters blessed,
In love's embrace, our souls find rest.
In every moment, life anew,
The spirit's gentle currents guide us through.

## **Fragments Gathered by Grace**

In silence deep, the heart does seek,
The threads of hope that softly speak.
With every tear, a promise flows,
In fragments gathered, love still grows.

The shattered pieces, bright like stars,
In darkness shine, erase the scars.
For grace abounds in weary nights,
And mends the soul with gentle lights.

Each prayer whispered in quiet grace,
Finds refuge in the warm embrace.
Though pathways twist and turn away,
The heart's true compass leads to stay.

Among the ruins of our quest,
A sacred calm, our souls find rest.
In every loss, a chance to gain,
Fragments of faith shall break the chain.

So let us gather in His name,
In humble hearts, ignite the flame.
For every shard, a story true,
In grace we find we are made new.

## The Prayer of the Weary Spirit

When shadows fall and spirits tire,
In whispered prayer, we lift desire.
The weight we carry, heavy still,
Yet in this moment, find His will.

With trembling hands and burdened hearts,
We seek the light where hope imparts.
In every sigh, a longing plea,
To find the strength to simply be.

The weary soul cries out in night,
Yet dawn will bring its tender light.
In gentle arms, He holds our fears,
And wipes away the bitter tears.

As faith endures through trials hard,
We find in love our true reward.
With every breath, we learn to trust,
In Him alone, our hearts adjust.

Let every heartbeat echo grace,
In quietude, we find our place.
For weary spirits, peace unfold,
In prayer, a refuge, pure and bold.

## Embracing Light in the Shadows

In shadows cast by doubts and fears,
We find the light that wipes the tears.
A gentle grace that calls us near,
Embracing warmth when all seems drear.

With every moment, darkness fades,
As faith directs and gently wades.
The light within, a sacred guide,
In trials faced, He walks beside.

Through valleys low and mountains tall,
We heed His voice, we heed His call.
In every heartbeat, love's embrace,
We find our way to His warm grace.

As stars emerge in twilight's kiss,
We glimpse the promise, purest bliss.
In shadows deep, we learn to see,
The light of hope that dwells in thee.

So let us journey hand in hand,
In faith, united, we will stand.
Embracing light, we rise anew,
In every moment, His love shines through.

# **The Crossroads of Love and Loss**

At the crossroads where heartbeats part,
Love meets loss, a tender art.
In every farewell, we feel the ache,
Yet in the grief, new paths we make.

With heavy hearts, we carry on,
For every dusk brings forth a dawn.
In memories held, we find the grace,
To navigate this sacred space.

As seasons change, so do our ways,
We learn to cherish fleeting days.
In love's embrace, we find the key,
To heal and grow, to simply be.

So let the tears fall where they will,
For every moment, time does steal.
Yet in the sorrow, joy does bloom,
A tapestry of life, consumed.

At this junction, faith will rise,
In every heart, love never dies.
For in the end, we understand,
Love's enduring touch will guide our hand.

## Chaucer's Reflection of Peace

In gardens lush, where silence grows,
A gentle breeze of mercy blows.
With each soft step on sacred ground,
In every heart, His love is found.

The river flows, a tranquil stream,
Where souls awaken from the dream.
With whispered prayers beneath the trees,
We find our solace in the breeze.

In humble homes, where echoes dwell,
Love's gentle touch, a sacred spell.
Through faith, our burdens start to fade,
In peace, His grace is freely laid.

As dawn unfolds, the light breaks through,
A canvas bright, each moment new.
With every heartbeat, we declare,
The Lord beside us, everywhere.

So let us walk, hand in hand strong,
With faith to guide us all along.
In harmony, our spirits soar,
For peace awaits, forevermore.

## The Holy Sands of Time

In grains of sand, our moments lie,
Each one a gift from the Most High.
We count them slow, we treasure fast,
For in His love, our shadows cast.

The clock ticks softly, wisdom speaks,
In every trial, the spirit seeks.
With every hour, a prayer ascends,
In stillness, where our journey bends.

From dawn to dusk, His light we crave,
A guide of grace, our souls to save.
In fleeting time, His will unfolds,
As stories of the faithful told.

So let us cherish, one by one,
The moments shared, as day is done.
In every breath, His presence near,
In holy sands, we cast our fear.

With every grain that slips away,
We find the strength to face the day.
For in His love, our hearts align,
Eternal truths in sands of time.

## Echoes of Faith in the Quiet

In twilight's hush, His whispers glide,
Through shadows deep, where hopes reside.
With every sigh, a prayer is borne,
In quiet nights, new faith is worn.

The stars alight, a distant grace,
Reflecting love in every space.
With every heartbeat, echoes sound,
In silence, we are tightly bound.

Through trials faced and challenges won,
We hear His voice, a gentle sun.
In solitude, our spirits rise,
To touch the vast and endless skies.

In sacred calm, His presence near,
We find our strength, we cast our fear.
In every moment, blessings flow,
In faith's embrace, our spirits glow.

So let us pause, in stillness dwell,
For in the quiet, all is well.
In echoes soft, our hearts align,
In faith's embrace, the stars will shine.

## Love's Restorative Rhythm

In gentle waves, love's rhythm sways,
Bringing hope to our weary days.
With every heartbeat, grace restores,
In sacred dance, our spirit soars.

The universe sings a tender song,
Reminding us where we belong.
In love's embrace, we find our way,
Through trials faced and shadows played.

With open hearts, we share the light,
In every moment, pure and bright.
Through laughter shared and tears we shed,
In love's soft glow, our fears are fed.

So let us move to love's sweet tune,
Beneath the stars and silver moon.
With every step, His grace we find,
A dance of love, forever kind.

In every heartbeat, every sigh,
We lift our souls toward the sky.
In love's embrace, we are made whole,
For in His light, we find our soul.

# Hymns of the Restored Soul

In shadows deep, my heart did ache,
Yet in the twilight, hope would wake.
With gentle grace, You pulled me near,
And whispered love, my doubt unclear.

The burdens heavy, I laid them down,
In Your embrace, I found my crown.
With every tear, You shaped my clay,
Your light within, my guiding way.

A hymn of joy now fills the air,
Each note a prayer, Your love laid bare.
In trials fierce, I stand assured,
For in Your arms, my soul is cured.

Together we walk, hand in hand,
Your presence is my promised land.
With every breath, I sing Your name,
Forever blessed, I feel the flame.

So let the world in chorus rise,
For in my heart, Your truth abides.
A song of light, my spirit whole,
In faith and love, the restored soul.

## The Light After the Darkness

In darkest nights, when hope seems lost,
I feel Your warmth, no matter the cost.
With gentle whispers, You call my name,
A guiding star, in love aflame.

Through tempest storms and trials grim,
Your light shines bright, when hearts grow dim.
Each step I take, I sense Your grace,
A beacon strong, in every place.

The dawn shall break, a promise new,
In every shadow, I see You true.
Your faithfulness, a steady thread,
In every tear, You steady my tread.

When all seems lost, a flicker glows,
Your presence blooms, like summer rose.
With every heartbeat, I trust the way,
For light will come, to guide my day.

So in the depths, my spirit soars,
In every struggle, hope restores.
The light of love dispels the night,
With You, dear Lord, my soul takes flight.

## Divine Hands I Trust

In every worry, in every fear,
Your hands are near, my heart you steer.
With fingerprints of love divine,
Through trials bold, I know You're mine.

Each burden heavy, I give to You,
Your strength, O Lord, makes all things new.
With gentle force, You mold my heart,
Divine Creator, skilled in art.

When storms arise and winds do howl,
Your steady hands, I trust, I prowl.
With faith I walk on waters wide,
For in Your grip, I will abide.

The path may twist, the shadows loom,
Yet in Your hands, I find my room.
A shelter strong, where love abounds,
In every whisper, comfort found.

So with each dawn, my spirit sings,
In every trial, my heart takes wings.
Divine hands guide, through thick and thin,
In trust I flourish, in You, I win.

## **Heartstrings Woven in Faith**

In every thread, our hearts entwined,
Through prayers whispered, love defined.
With gentle hands, You weave the peace,
In faith's embrace, all fears release.

When trials strike, our bond grows strong,
In faith, O Lord, we will belong.
Together we rise, though storms may rage,
In trust we find our turning page.

Each heartbeat echoes Your sacred vow,
In moments sweet, with You, I bow.
With every smile, a grace bestowed,
In faith and love, our hearts bestowed.

As seasons change, our spirits blend,
With every prayer, on You we depend.
These heartstrings tie, unbroken flow,
In love, in faith, our spirits glow.

So together, Lord, we journey through,
With heartstrings woven, ever true.
In every step, I feel You near,
In faith and love, I banish fear.

## Beneath the Veil of Solitude

In silence deep, the heart does kneel,
Awash in whispers, divine and real.
The stars align, in shadows cast,
A balm for wounds, the peace to last.

In stillness found, the spirit soars,
Where echoes fade, and love restores.
Beneath the veils, a sacred trust,
We rise anew, from dust to dust.

The world retreats; the soul draws near,
In solitude, we face the fear.
With faith as guide, we journey on,
Through night's embrace, until the dawn.

A tranquil heart, a gentle hand,
In solitude, we understand.
The quiet voice, the whisper sweet,
In His presence, our lives complete.

With every breath, a prayer we share,
Among the stars, beyond compare.
For in this space, we learn to see,
The beauty found in being free.

## The Altar of Brokenness

Upon the heights, the shadows fall,
In brokenness, we heed the call.
With shattered dreams, our spirits bend,
At this altar, we find a friend.

Each tender scar, a tale unfolds,
Of love, of loss, of hearts consoled.
In grief's embrace, our burdens shared,
Through unity, our souls repaired.

In every tear, a prayer ascends,
For in surrender, our heart mends.
Beneath the weight, a grace ignites,
In darkness deep, we find our light.

The broken pieces, they fit as one,
Revealing grace, a life begun.
With every step, we stand restored,
At this altar, sweet love poured.

In offering hands, we break the bread,
Of brokenness, new life is bred.
Together we rise, in faith we stand,
At the altar of His gentle hand.

## Restoration through Faith's Embrace

In faith we find the path ahead,
With every tear, our hearts are fed.
Through trials faced and storms we brave,
The light of hope begins to save.

Each step we take, though fraught with pain,
Reveals a strength that breaks the chain.
In every struggle, grace abounds,
Through shattered dreams, true love is found.

With open hearts, we seek the way,
In every night, we long for day.
Through whispered prayers, our spirits rise,
Restoration blooms beneath the skies.

Like morning dew, fresh and clear,
Faith's gentle whispers calm our fear.
In unity, we lean to trust,
Restored by love, through faith, we must.

The journey long, yet not alone,
In every heartbeat, love is known.
Through trials faced, our hope shall hold,
In faith's embrace, our lives unfold.

# A Soul's Pilgrimage to Wholeness

A pilgrimage, the heart does face,
To seek the light, to find our place.
Through winding paths and shadowed trails,
To wholeness found, our spirit hails.

Beneath the sky, with every breath,
We sow the seeds of life from death.
In every step, a truth unfolds,
A story rich, through trials bold.

With every tear, a blessing flows,
In darkest nights, our spirit grows.
Through storms we walk, unafraid to tread,
For in this journey, hope is bred.

In gentle whispers, we hear the call,
Awakening the heart in all.
Through valleys low and mountains high,
Our souls ascend, we learn to fly.

With open arms, we greet the dawn,
In wholeness found, our fears are gone.
A sacred quest, forever bold,
A soul's pilgrimage, a joy retold.

## Sacred Echoes of Inner Peace

In stillness, hearts begin to mend,
Whispers of love, on every bend.
Light dances gently on the soul,
Guiding us softly toward the whole.

Each breath a prayer of deep refrain,
In the silence, we release the pain.
Sacred echoes fill the night,
As dawn awakens with pure light.

The path is steep, yet we ascend,
With faith and courage, we will defend.
Inner peace, our guiding star,
Leading us home, no matter how far.

In unity, we find our grace,
Embracing all with a warm embrace.
Let kindness bloom in every heart,
For love will always play its part.

With gentle steps on sacred ground,
In every moment, grace is found.
We walk together, hand in hand,
United by the divine command.

## Gathering Shattered Dreams

In the quiet, fragments glow,
Pieces scattered, yearning to grow.
We lift our eyes to the sky above,
Finding strength in sacred love.

Each sorrow sings a bittersweet tune,
In the light of the gentle moon.
Gathering hopes that once seemed lost,
We build anew, no matter the cost.

With open hearts, we weave the threads,
Binding together what once was shed.
In every dream that stirs the night,
There lies a chance to find the light.

Through trials faced and lessons learned,
In every scar, the spirit earned.
We gather strength from shattered finds,
As we seek what the heart reminds.

Each vision sparks a sacred fire,
Reigning hope that will inspire.
Together, we rise from the seams,
In the power of our gathering dreams.

Above the storms, our voices blend,
Creating beauty that will not end.
We lift each other, stand as one,
In the dawn, we are reborn.

## A Glimpse into Divine Wholeness

In sacred space, the heart aligns,
Dancing lightly on the lines.
Glancing toward the heavens high,
Where all our truths, like stars, lie.

Each moment brings a glimpse of grace,
Reflecting love in every face.
As rivers flow through valleys near,
We sense divinity drawing near.

With every prayer, the spirit sings,
Connecting us to all living things.
In tender whispers, wisdom speaks,
Filling the void that each one seeks.

Dissolving doubt, we find our way,
Embracing light to guide each day.
In the depths of silence, we see,
A glimpse of wholeness, truly free.

The tapestry of life unfolds,
In every thread, the love it holds.
With open hearts, we dare to find,
The essence of the divine, intertwined.

Through every challenge, hope will bloom,
Casting out shadows, dispelling gloom.
In the unity of spirit's call,
Awake, rejoice, for love is all.

## Recovery Through Sacred Prayer

In the hush of night, we kneel in grace,
Seeking solace in this sacred place.
Each whispered word, a healing balm,
Wrapping our spirits in peaceful calm.

With every prayer, the heart's released,
In the embrace of love, we're least.
Finding comfort in faith's sweet embrace,
Together, we journey through the space.

Through trials faced, our voices rise,
In unity, we reach the skies.
The strength of many heals the soul,
With every prayer, we become whole.

In sacred circles, hope ignites,
Turning darkness into lights.
Recovery blooms like flowers in spring,
With love and faith, we find our wing.

Each heartbeat echoes the sacred sound,
In collective love, our peace is found.
As we surrender to the divine,
We rise again, our spirits shine.

Through prayerful hearts, we share the weight,
In sacred moments, we cultivate.
Together, we heal, we learn, we grow,
In the sacred flow, our spirits glow.

# A Psalm for Weary Souls

In the valley low, I seek Your light,
With trembling hands, I lift my plight.
Each burden carried, heavy and worn,
Yet through my tears, I find a dawn.

O gentle Shepherd, lead me near,
With every echo, calm my fear.
In quiet moments, hear my plea,
Restore my spirit, set it free.

When shadows loom, and hope feels lost,
Remind me, Lord, of love's true cost.
You walk beside me, every day,
In Your embrace, I find my way.

The road is long, with trials faced,
Yet in Your grace, I find my place.
With every step, I rise anew,
A journey crafted, just for you.

So lift my heart with songs of praise,
In weary nights and brighter days.
For in my weakness, strength is shown,
In the embrace of love, I'm home.

## **In the Sanctuary of Forgiveness**

In moments lost, where shadows dwell,
I find a peace, my soul to quell.
Your mercy flows like rivers wide,
In Your sanctuary, I can abide.

With open arms, You draw me near,
In every sin, You calm my fear.
Each whispered prayer, a gentle tide,
In the sanctuary, I confide.

Forgive my past, O Lord divine,
In every heartache, You design.
A tapestry of grace and love,
Woven together from above.

As dawn breaks bright, my heart restored,
In gratefulness, I lift my sword.
To fight the battles brave and true,
In the shelter of Your heart, anew.

Within these walls, no shame remains,
Your love, O Lord, my spirit gains.
With every breath, I choose to live,
In the grace, my heart you give.

## **The Breath of New Beginnings**

From ashes rise, the dawn is near,
With open hearts, we cast our fear.
A breath of hope, the start anew,
In every moment, I trust in You.

The chains of sorrow, broken free,
In Your embrace, I learn to see.
A path of purpose, bright and bold,
In every story yet untold.

Awaken dreams that long have slept,
In faith, I step where shadows crept.
With every heartbeat, wings take flight,
A journey blessed by purest light.

Through trials faced and battles won,
Your hand in mine, we journey on.
With each new dawn, my heart takes wing,
In every breath, a song I sing.

As seasons change and time unfolds,
I greet the new with heart of gold.
For in Your Spirit, life I find,
The breath of hope, forever kind.

## Shattered Yet Shine

In fragments laid upon the floor,
A heart once whole, now aches for more.
Yet in the cracks, Your light does seep,
A promise held, a love to keep.

With every tear, a story told,
In shadows deep, I find my gold.
Your grace transforms the broken pieces,
In every loss, my spirit increases.

I rise like stars from endless night,
A testament of hope and light.
From shattered dreams, new visions grow,
In Your embrace, my courage flows.

Though wounds remain, I bear the scars,
A canvas painted by the stars.
In every struggle, I shall find,
The strength to love, the grace to bind.

So let the world see strength within,
For in my heart, the light has been.
Shattered yet whole, I stand and shine,
A child of love, eternally thine.

## Redemption's Gentle Whisper

In the silence where shadows lie,
He speaks softly to the weary soul.
A promise of hope, sweet and spry,
Washing away the burdens we hold.

With every breath, His mercy flows,
A balm for the heart that has strayed.
In His embrace, true comfort grows,
In the darkest night, we are laid.

He gathers the lost, the broken, the meek,
In arms of love, we find our place.
Redemption speaks, tender and weak,
Whispering joy in His gentle grace.

Through trials and storms, we rise anew,
The weight of sin, He gently lifts.
In every tear, His light shines through,
An echo of love—the greatest gift.

So let the heart sing out in praise,
For every moment, He's the guide.
In redemption's breath, we find our ways,
In His tender whispers, we abide.

## **Beneath Heaven's Wings**

When the night falls, dark and deep,
We seek shelter from fear and woe.
Under Heaven's wings, we safely leap,
Finding peace where the wild winds blow.

With every heartbeat, grace descends,
A shield of faith, our souls ignite.
In prayer, our spirit mends,
Unified in love, shining bright.

The trials that seem to never cease,
Are but whispers in the grand design.
In struggle, we find a sacred peace,
Trusting in the plan that is divine.

So lift your eyes to the skies above,
For hope is born within the strife.
Beneath those wings, the pulse of love,
Guiding us through this fleeting life.

As dawn breaks forth, all shadows flee,
We stand renewed in light so clear.
Beneath Heaven's wings, together we be,
In harmony, banishing fear.

# **The Garden of Second Chances**

In the quiet grove where dreams are sown,
Seeds of mercy begin to sprout.
The garden beckons, a chance to atone,
With every bloom, there's hope to tout.

In every heart, a story blooms,
Of storms endured and battles fought.
Among the petals, grace consumes,
Nurturing the seeds of love that's sought.

Each withered stem, a tale of loss,
Yet new life springs with each dawn's light.
With gentle hands, we bear the cross,
Forgiveness whispers in the night.

As fragrance mingles in the air,
Wounds are healed in vibrant hues.
The garden thrives, a sacred prayer,
Home to the hopes we dare to choose.

So let us wander, hand in hand,
Through paths adorned with tender grace.
In the garden, forever we stand,
Embracing life in this holy place.

## **Divine Grace in Broken Places**

In shattered dreams, where sorrow dwells,
A light emerges through every crack.
Divine grace flows and softly tells,
That even broken can find the track.

Through weary days and silent nights,
His love will cradle the wounded heart.
In every fall, there's strength in fights,
Through darkness, a brand-new start.

The scars we bear are testament true,
Of battles won and courage found.
In broken places, grace breaks through,
Transforming loss to sacred ground.

So lift your gaze, O weary soul,
For beauty rises from the dust.
In every fragment, we find our whole,
In faith, in love, in hope—trust.

In every tear that falls like rain,
A blessing blooms, a chance to grow.
In broken places, we'll rise again,
For divine grace is what we sow.

# Seraphic Touch of Healing

In shadows deep, where sorrow lies,
The seraphs sing beneath the skies.
Their gentle wings, a balm so pure,
Bring peace and hope, our hearts assure.

A whisper soft, a holy breeze,
With every sigh, our souls appease.
In sacred light, the spirit mends,
A touch of love that never ends.

Through trials faced and burdens borne,
Our faith ignites, the dawn is sworn.
In every tear, a lesson grows,
The healing hands of grace bestows.

As flowers bloom from winter's hold,
The seraph's touch, a story told.
With every heartbeat, every prayer,
We find the strength to rise, aware.

So let the light through darkness flow,
In seraphic grace, our spirits glow.
Together bound, in love we stand,
With healing hearts, we join His hand.

## Sacred Threads of Forgiveness

In woven strands of sacred grace,
Forgiveness blooms in every place.
With open hearts, we mend the seam,
A tapestry, a holy dream.

Each thread a tale of sorrow past,
In love's embrace, we find it cast.
Through trials faced, we learn to rise,
With mercy wrapped in gentle ties.

The weight of anger, set aside,
In sacred trust, we shall abide.
As light breaks through the darkest night,
Forgiveness shines, a guiding light.

In every heart, the power flows,
To weave anew, to heal, to close.
The fabric strong, in unity,
A sacred bond, our legacy.

So let the threads of grace entwine,
In forgiveness, our souls align.
With every stitch, a chance to mend,
The sacred thread that knows no end.

## The Altar of Rebirth

At dawn we gather, hope in sight,
The altar gleams with morning light.
In silent prayers, we lay to rest,
The dreams long lost, we seek our quest.

From ashes rise, the spirit's call,
In every heart, we hear it all.
With courage found, we shed the past,
And step into the light at last.

In waves of grace, our burdens fade,
The altar stands, our fears cascaded.
With open arms, the heavens smile,
Inviting all to walk the aisle.

As souls reborn, the journey starts,
With every step, we mend our hearts.
Embrace the change, the love bestowed,
The altar calls, we are enfolded.

In every moment, life renewed,
At the altar, faith pursued.
With joy, we rise to bless the day,
Through rebirth's light, we find our way.

## **Celestial Embrace of Redemption**

Beneath the stars, we find our grace,
In every heart, a sacred space.
With arms extended, love draws near,
The celestial embrace, calm our fear.

In trials faced, we seek the light,
Redemption comes in darkest night.
Through every fall, we learn to fly,
With faith that roots, our spirits high.

The heavens sing, a song of peace,
In every soul, a sweet release.
With gentle hands, our sorrows lift,
In love, we find the greatest gift.

Through tears of joy, the spirit soars,
With every breath, our hearts explore.
In every moment, grace abounds,
Celestial whispers, joy surrounds.

So let us walk this path of light,
In redemption's grace, we find our sight.
With every step, our hearts aligned,
In celestial love, we all unwind.

## **The Weight of Glory Restored**

In shadows deep, we seek Your grace,
A whisper soft in a fearful place.
Through trials faced, we rise anew,
Your glory shines, our spirits true.

With heavy hearts, we lift our eyes,
To You, O Lord, the great and wise.
In every pain, Your love remains,
Through weary paths, our faith sustains.

The weight of glory breaks the night,
In darkest moments, You are light.
Your promise firm, our hearts restore,
In silence deep, we long for more.

From ashes, hope begins to grow,
The seeds of faith You freely sow.
In beauty carved from trials bare,
Your loving hands our souls repair.

Rejoice, O hearts, for dawn shall break,
In trust we find what's at stake.
For in Your arms, we find our peace,
The weight of glory grants release.

## Ever Present in the Brokenness

In brokenness, we lift our plea,
O Lord, embrace our misery.
Your gentle hand, it guides us near,
In every loss, You wipe each tear.

In darkest days, You draw us close,
A tender heart, our only host.
Among the ruins, hope will rise,
Your love, a balm, our spirit ties.

You know our pain, each heavy sigh,
O hear our cries, as we reply.
Ever present in our grief,
You bring us solace, sweet relief.

And as we walk through valleys low,
Your light will guide us, ever so.
In brokenness, our hearts will find,
A love that heals, a strength combined.

So in our trials, we shall abide,
Your faithfulness, our faithful guide.
In every step, through joy and strife,
You breathe in us, eternal life.

# Beauty Born of Trials

In trials fierce, the soul awakes,
Through pain and loss, the heart remakes.
From shattered dreams, new visions rise,
In darkest nights, Your light supplies.

We bear the burdens, honor each scar,
In every struggle, You are never far.
Your presence felt in hardest days,
Reminds us of Your righteous ways.

A tapestry of grace is spun,
In every heartache, we're not undone.
For beauty gleaned from broken earth,
Reveals the glory of our worth.

Each trial faced, a lesson learned,
In faithfulness, our hearts have turned.
To trust in You amidst the strife,
For beauty born reveals true life.

When storms arise, we stand in peace,
Our eyes fixed high, our fears release.
For in the trials, we can see,
The beauty formed, Your majesty.

## The Covenant of Renewal

Amidst the ruins, grace descends,
A covenant where love transcends.
In faithful hearts, we pledge anew,
O God of hope, we cling to You.

Through seasons change, Your word remains,
In every loss, through every gain.
A promise held, forever true,
In darkest days, we're sheltered too.

With open hands, we give our all,
In joy and sorrow, we heed the call.
For in the giving, life shall bloom,
In hearts that yearn, dispelling gloom.

A steadfast bond, a sacred vow,
We walk in faith, our heads unbowed.
This covenant deep, unshakeable grace,
In every trial, Your love we trace.

So lead us forth, O Shepherd kind,
With hearts aligned, our spirits bind.
In restoration, we shall thrive,
The covenant of renewal, alive.

## **The Promise of Restoration**

In shadows deep, our spirits weep,
Yet hope ignites a flame to keep.
The whispers of grace, calm the storm,
A heart anew, in love's warm form.

From ashes rise, the weary soul,
With faith restored, we'll be made whole.
The dawn shall break, our fears take flight,
In sacred trust, we find the light.

## Wings of Faith on Broken Paths

When trials weigh and doubt ensues,
In prayer's embrace, we'll glean the truths.
With every step, our hearts take wing,
On broken roads, His love will sing.

The path is rough, yet grace abounds,
In whispered hopes, His peace surrounds.
Through darkest nights, our spirits soar,
Together, we will rise and more.

## The Symphony of the Humble Heart

With gentle notes, the heart will play,
In humble grace, we find our way.
Each kindness shared, a melody,
That echoes through eternity.

In silence sweet, we tune our souls,
To love's embrace, our spirits whole.
A symphony composed of light,
In harmony, we take our flight.

**Love's Resplendent Revival**

In quiet corners, love ignites,
A spark divine, in darkest nights.
With open hands and hearts so pure,
We rise anew, in faith secure.

Through trials faced, and sorrows steep,
Love's tender call wakes hearts from sleep.
In every tear, a blessing found,
In love's revival, we are crowned.

# A Journey Through Sacred Silence

In the hush where spirits dwell,
Whispers of the ancients swell.
Hearts open in the quiet night,
Seeking solace, thirsting for light.

Footsteps trace the sacred ground,
In stillness, grace is found.
With every breath, we rise and fall,
The voice of God, a gentle call.

Through shadows deep, we find our way,
In prayerful pause, the truth will stay.
Love unspoken lingers here,
In sacred silence, we draw near.

A journey wrought with joy and pain,
In gratitude, our hearts remain.
Bound by faith, we walk as one,
Underneath the shining sun.

Each moment rests in fragrant peace,
In love's embrace, our fears release.
The still small voice, a guiding ray,
In the silence, we learn to pray.

## The Pathway to Wholeness

On the road of humble grace,
We find ourselves in sacred space.
Each step taken, a gentle guide,
With open hearts and arms spread wide.

Through valleys low and mountains high,
We rise together, spirits nigh.
In unity, our strength we share,
For love's embrace is everywhere.

Every wound becomes a light,
Transforming shadows into bright.
With every struggle, peace is won,
As we walk towards the risen sun.

In the journey, life unfolds,
In every story, grace retold.
With faith as our unwavering guide,
We find wholeness on this ride.

Hand in hand, through thick and thin,
The sacred song, our hearts begin.
Together, we rise, we grow,
In love's embrace, we come to know.

## **Beneath the Veil of Sorrow**

In shadows cast by grief's embrace,
We seek the light, a fleeting trace.
Beneath the veil, the heartache lies,
Where hope is born, and the spirit flies.

Tears like rivers carve the stone,
Yet in the dark, we are not alone.
With whispered prayers, we stand tall,
In sorrow's depths, we heed the call.

The weight of loss, a sacred lore,
In silent moments, we explore.
Through every heart, a story shared,
In love's embrace, we are prepared.

Through brokenness, our spirits mend,
With faith that doubt cannot suspend.
For in the night, our souls ignite,
Transcending pain, we seek the light.

Beneath the veil, our spirits rise,
In unity, the heart replies.
Through sorrow, we discover grace,
In each embrace, a warm embrace.

## Psalms of the Gathered Heart

In unison, our voices blend,
A sacred song, we offer, send.
With joyful hearts, we lift our praise,
In gratitude, we spend our days.

From every corner, praises flow,
In every smile, the love we know.
Together, we weave a tapestry,
Of hope and light, eternally.

Each psalm a thread, a sacred bond,
In every heart, we respond.
With every beat, our spirits soar,
In gatherings rich, we find our core.

Through trials faced and battles won,
We gather strength, we are as one.
In community, our faith ignites,
Illuminating darkest nights.

So let our songs rise high and free,
In every note, sweet harmony.
With every heart, forever part,
Together, we sing, a gathered heart.

## The Covenant of Healing

In whispers soft, He speaks of grace,
Binding wounds in a holy place.
The promise shines in tender light,
Restoring hope, dispelling night.

With every tear, love's gentle hand,
He leads us to a promised land.
Through trials dark, His comfort flows,
In every heart, His mercy grows.

The broken find their strength anew,
In healing hands, the old made true.
A covenant forged in sacred trust,
In Him alone, our hearts are just.

Rejoice in faith, the spirit sings,
For every wound, His healing brings.
The path of love, a guiding star,
With Him beside, we've come so far.

## Rays of Mercy in the Storm

When storms arise and shadows fall,
In Him we seek, our Savior's call.
The tempest rages, hearts are worn,
Yet mercy shines, a light reborn.

Through darkest nights, we find our way,
His loving arms, our safe array.
With every wave, His voice we hear,
"Fear not, my child, I am still near."

In trials faced, our spirits soar,
He calms the seas, and opens doors.
Each tear a pearl in heaven's hold,
In faith, we find our hearts unfold.

The rays of mercy pierce the gloom,
Revealing hope, dispelling doom.
With every breath, we trust His plan,
In every storm, the love we span.

## **Resurgence in His Grace**

From ashes rise, a fervent flame,
In grace renewed, we bear His name.
With each new dawn, redemption calls,
In open hearts, His love enthralls.

The weary find their strength restored,
In prayerful whispers, His word adored.
In shadows deep, His light breaks through,
In every soul, His essence true.

The chains that bound, now gently fall,
In His embrace, we hear the call.
To live anew in joy and peace,
From grace to grace, our hearts increase.

Resurgence blooms in every heart,
With love unbound, we shall not part.
Together bound in sacred trust,
In Him, we rise, from dust to dust.

# The Returning of Lost Spirits

In wandering paths, we lose our way,
Yet grace, like dawn, brings forth the day.
The lost are called from shadows deep,
In His embrace, our spirits leap.

With gentle hands, He lifts us high,
Restoring dreams, as eagles fly.
The prodigal finds joy once more,
In open arms, love's sweet restore.

Through valleys low, and mountains steep,
His promise true, our souls to keep.
No heart too lost, no life too far,
For in His eyes, we're all a star.

The returning souls, united sing,
In gratitude, our praises ring.
In every heart, a sacred fire,
To dwell in love, our hearts' desire.

# From Ashes to Eternal Light

In shadows deep, we find our grace,
From ashes risen, we seek His face.
The fire of spirit, forever bright,
Guides us onward to eternal light.

With hearts aflame, we walk this road,
Casting off burdens, lightening our load.
Each step in faith, a holy song,
From ashes to glory, we all belong.

Through trials faced, the soul refined,
In darkest hours, His love aligned.
With every tear, a lesson learned,
From ashes we rise, the heart discerned.

As dawn awakens, hope starts to shine,
In every moment, His will, divine.
We gather strength, hand in hand,
From ashes to light, we firmly stand.

In reverence deep, we shed our plight,
Transformed by faith, we claim the night.
Eternal whispers lead us near,
From ashes to light, no more fear.

## The Prayer of the Weary

Oh Lord, hear my weary plea,
In the stillness, set me free.
With burdens heavy upon my heart,
In Your embrace, I seek a start.

Through trials faced, my spirit wanes,
In humble prayer, release my chains.
Guide my footsteps on this way,
A flicker of hope, come what may.

In quiet moments, I raise my hand,
To feel Your touch, to understand.
Restore my strength, renew my fight,
Oh Lord, lead me to the light.

Each tear that falls, a seed of grace,
In the garden of love, I find my place.
With whispered prayers, I break the night,
Oh Lord, hold me through this plight.

Together we rise, from shadows deep,
In faith, our promises we keep.
Remove the weariness from my soul,
Oh Lord, as You make me whole.

## Sacred Waters of Healing

In sacred waters, we find our peace,
Let troubled hearts begin to cease.
Flowing gently, a calming stream,
In the embrace of His love, we dream.

Each ripple tells of grace anew,
As living waters bring forth the true.
With every drop, a blessing falls,
In sacred silence, the spirit calls.

Come, be washed in these healing waves,
For every sorrow, the heart it saves.
With faith as deep as ocean's might,
In sacred waters, we find our light.

Here in this place, we lay our fears,
Beneath the surface, release our tears.
A journey inward, our souls ignite,
In sacred waters, we reunite.

Let streams of mercy flow through my soul,
In every moment, make me whole.
In sacred waters, I find my song,
With hearts united, we all belong.

## **A Pilgrimage of the Spirit**

On this path, my spirit roams,
In searching hearts, I find my home.
With every step, a purpose clear,
A pilgrimage, with faith sincere.

Through valleys low and mountains high,
In nature's whispers, I hear Your sigh.
Guided by stars, through night's embrace,
Each moment feels a touch of grace.

In solitude's depth, wisdom unfolds,
The journey rich, as truth beholds.
With open arms, I greet the dawn,
In this pilgrimage, I am reborn.

Together we walk, both near and far,
Under the watching, guiding star.
Through trials faced, we'll not despair,
For in His love, we find our prayer.

As spirits rise, our voices blend,
On this holy road, we shall not end.
A pilgrimage of love and light,
In every heart, His truth ignites.

Milton Keynes UK
Ingram Content Group UK Ltd.
UKHW020043271124
451585UK00012B/1020

9 789916 898604